Kudos
For Ebb & Flow

"A brilliant blend of confessional intimacy, naturalism, magic, humanism, Susan Sweetland Garay's poetry collection, Ebb & Flow, feels just as its title implies. The verse herein is life-affirming, life-giving, while carrying serious truths that devour old ideas in favor of constant renewal. Garay appears to give wholly of herself among these pages, offering something just short of a memoir, presented in vivid snapshots that bond reader and poet in unspoken friendship. This collection is about love, finding it within and without, and learning how to hold it, gently and safely, as to not break it."

– **Nate Ragolia**, editor of BONED: A collection of skeletal writings, author of *The Retroactivist* and *There You Feel Free.*

"Tip O'Neil once said that "all politics is local"; what I have learned again from Susie Sweetland Garay is that the same can be said of poetry. While I have never been to her corner of the world I feel, through her poems, that I know the landscape of northwestern Oregon as though a friend has guided me through it: she has shown me where to pause to discover its signatures, it's indelible traits and touches. But more than this, I know her Oregon because Susie has made it a fixture of her intimate thoughts, her wishes and words of love and advice to those who matter most. But just as moving is how the verses in her book are shaped, perhaps in equal measure, by the terrestrial contours she has made a part of herself. Ebb & Flow is a voice, one which I will not forget."

– **Jeremy Nathan Marks**, a Canada-based American essayist and poet

"Susie Sweetland Garay's *Ebb & Flow* is a collection steeped in the power of memory, both in your mind and in your muscles. It is a testament to nostalgia, to coming close to the things we fear and in that moment daring to keep our eyes open. Writing about the body, bones, the earth, and motherhood, she weaves a narrative of forgiveness and compassion reminding us that we are beautiful because we are temporary. These are poems about truth and mercy and the surprising hope that sprouts from death – the way a good wind can wipe us clean. Lyrical and haunting, Garay's work cuts to the core of our needs reminding us that, "So much can change when you ask the right questions."

– **Ally Malinenko,** author of *Fitting the Ocean in Your Mouth*

Ebb & Flow

By Susan Sweetland Garay

Ebb& Flow
Copyright © 2018 by Susan Sweetland Garay

All rights reserved. No part of this book may be used or reproduced in any manner whatsoever without written permission except in the case of brief quotations embodied in critical articles or reviews. For information address: Boho Books, 36179 S. Sawtell Road, Molalla, OR 97038.

ISBN: 978-0-9988455-4-8 (paperback)
       978-0-9988455-5-5 (ebook)

Printed in the United States of America

Cover Photo: Shutterstock

Interior Photos: Susan Sweetland Garay

For Aria

"It may be that when we no longer know which way to go that we have come to our real journey. The mind that is not baffled is not employed. The impeded stream is the one that sings."

Wendell Berry

Table of Contents

Waxing

Ancient Corners	1
Motherhood	3
The Question	4
Ebb & Flow	5
Pinpricks	7
Skin	8
Summer Days	9
Rise	10
Thanksgiving	12
Go Softly	14
Unearth	15
Putting the Baby to Sleep	16
Grandfather	17
The Continuity of Things	18
Poverty Bend Road	20
Muted	22
Rib Cage	24
Learning to Sing	25
Layers	26
Death in the Country	27
Bones on the Brain	28
Optimists Underneath	29
Cooking Dinner Together in the Late Summer or Early Fall	30
Unmade	31
Leap Day	32
Small Corner	33
I Dreamt that I Died	34
The First Time We Hear the Coyotes After a Long Winter	35
Ritual	36
Walks	37
The Way	39

Waning

Lantern Light...42
Inverted..44
Orange Peels...46
Needles..48
Messages to Myself..49
A Night in Harvest...51
Icicle Creek...53
Cyclical..54
The Wet Green Forest..55
Distraction..57
A Fast Burn or a Slow Unfolding..................................58
The Ferns..59
Chapel..61
Eclipse Season...62
Dreaming of the Dead and the Not Yet Born.............63
Underwater Life..65
Sun Break..66
West..67
Blank Pages...69
Breakfast..70
Listening..71
Tracks...73
4th of July... 74
The Next Phase...75
Reason Enough...77
All Directions..78
Comfort..79
Wind Storm...80
Sunrise..81
Ask..82
The Necessity of Rage..84
Speak Up..86
Quench...88
Acknowledgements
Author Bio

Waxing

Ancient Corners

In a river on the fourth of July,
submerged to my waist in icy water,
this weary and neglected body
does not feel imperfect.

I sink down into my hips
stretch
feel my skin
feel the water moving around me
cold and rushing.

It finds
ancient walls
and corners
page numbers

with moss growing
and flowers coming through the cracks
reaching for the sun.

We drove past a charred hillside to get here,
so recently burned I could still smell the smoke.
But the black ground did not seem sad or lifeless,
instead I could almost see it breathing deeply as it rested.

I used to know the way,
but now I have forgotten

and I wonder what else I have forgotten
from when I was a tree
with my roots
winding
down
into the
lovely,
nourishing
earth.

Susan Sweetland Garay

When other trees and ferns and mushrooms
whispered to me

and I understood their language
and the movements of their leaves.

Motherhood

I want to make things perfect for her
in a way that is impossible,
that is only an illusion.

But knowing that doesn't
make the desire any less,

it just makes me obsessed
with an impossible task,

as perhaps
all mothers
are.

Susan Sweetland Garay

The Question

I have asked
so many times
thinking that maybe
the answer
would change,

are we safe to hope?
to trust that right will be
the outcome?

No my child,
we are never safe,
but we still must hope
and hope and
hope.

There is no other answer.

Ebb & Flow

Remember there is
beauty in roundness
and bounty

in a body
that has been indulged,

that has produced life.

The forest does not fast,
the ocean would not turn away
a child who is hungry

there is space enough and all are welcome.

I am a record keeper -
a memory keeper
with no memory.

So I try to record
in ink and silver
and hunks of bone,

but chances of success
are slim.

So we mend what we can
and let go of what we can't

and for God's sake stop buying
to try to fill the void.

I breathe deep
and teach my daughter
to do the same.

Susan Sweetland Garay

Her frustration
is hard for me to bear,
but I bear it.

I am the ebb and the flow.

I dream
but cling tightly
to what's real, always
afraid to lose my
grip.

I believe in plenty
but cannot share.

I crave stillness
but I am not still.

I am the optimist
who will not die,
who cannot sleep.

I do not wait to use what is cherished
I do not wait
I dive in.

I change
though I constantly
resist changing.

I want to be light
but the heaviness
remains.

I want to soften
but remain
hard.

Pinpricks

My pelvic bowl holds us
like the ocean at night

beautiful and dark
frightening and
full of mystery

and secrets
of creation
and power

with so much hidden
just underneath.

Starlight
shines through
in pinpricks

illuminating just enough.

She fantasizes about freedom
but does not climb down from her cage.

When she is angry
she speaks again and again
until she is heard.

She makes the hard decisions

and walks slowly
through the space of quiet
and discomfort and
remembering.

Skin

She goes down for her nap peacefully
while I watch hopefully on the monitor,
soaking up every second.

Quietly I sneak outside and feel the warm sun
on my sensitive skin which protects me and carries
a record of my sometimes difficult past.

Scars and freckles and sun spots
collected slowly over the years.

I tend to my plants
pulling off dead leaves
and carefully save
each living broken piece.

I lay them down gently
amidst dark brown dirt.
I take care to give enough
but not too much water.

I watch things grow to try to heal
a part of me that was broken.

Turns out I have more patience than I thought.

When she wakes we both
go happily back outside.

Summer days

My summer days switch between
the monotony and business of the office
and the muted beauty
and occasional ache
of days at home
in the heat
with my
darling
and
strong willed
daughter.

She loves to tell me her secrets,
to take me by the shoulders
and lean in close

so she can get just the right angle to
look me in the eye and
make sure I am
paying proper
attention.

I do my best to listen and understand.

We mark both the end
and the beginning
of things.

We owe it to our daughters
and all the mothers who came
before us.

We are patient
and when we are lucky
the chaos turns to calm.

Rise

I look out the window of an old brick building
and the sky is full of helicopters.

There is a gust of wind
and suddenly they all rise
at once.

So much can change
when you ask the right
questions.

So I return to what I know,
to my reasons,
which can be so hard to hold on to,

but I find them
and then I
dig in
and
hold tight.

The most beautiful mystery
is in how creation occurs,
how elements combine
inside us
to make something
separate
and new.

Ebb & Flow

Lately I find bits of poems everywhere
on the backs of a grocery list
or typed as a note on my phone,
who knows when I wrote them
or what that moment looked like.

We act clumsily
but it is so much better
than to not act at all.

Susan Sweetland Garay

Thanksgiving

On this day of thanksgiving
I will give thanks
for clouds
and the linings of clouds,

for bare feet in grass
and painted toenails.
For blues above and greens below,
for trees (oh trees, I could write
an entire book giving thanks for trees)

and birds and baby animals of all kinds.
For taste and all things good and edible.
For open eyes and hands closed around hands.

For distances
and coming closer
and time and learning
to be patient when it is
so so hard to wait.

For books and those who write them,
for a warm fire or cold drink,
for everything natural
and brown and dirty
that gets under your fingernails.

For hellos and gravel roads
and a first glimpse of a new place.
For trust and all it leads to
and for old friends.

Ebb & Flow

For passionate fighting
and loves of all kinds,
for goodbyes
and family eating around a table,

even if a few of you wish you were
somewhere else,
thank God that you are there
and here and wherever you will be tomorrow.

Go Softly

We all expand and retract
with the seasons

and today
on this first day of summer
I am expanding.

We shed skin like snakes and become tender
until time passes and it builds up again,

but I want to stay tender.

The answer
to most any question
is practice,

and here too I think
it is the answer.

I am defined by motherhood

but am unsure what the consequences will be.
Perhaps too much softness.

We named our cat
after the most flawed
character in a favorite show

and now every time we say
his name in love or anger
we are reminded of
his namesake
and where his
softness took him.

Unearth

Once
I went into a
rocky cave
carpeted
in green.
It was dark
and damp and
time sped up there.

We all feel lost sometimes
but the road is before us
and none of us want to stand still.

I think I write to
uncover the maps
I know are all around me,
to unearth what is already there.

It's June now and suddenly
everything seems
to be opening.

Susan Sweetland Garay

Putting the Baby to Sleep

Though I have heard it
a thousand times
I am still surprised
by the miraculous sound
of her voice.

She babbles before
she falls asleep,
telling me stories
from her day and
kicking her legs joyfully
as though running some
terrific race.

She falls asleep
suddenly and with
a fist full of my hair.

Grandfather

I heard stories
of his harshness,
but never felt it -

how could I have,
I was just a little girl,
always able to charm him
into opening the jar
of candy

even when it
was only minutes
before dinner.

Susan Sweetland Garay

The Continuity of Things

Let us talk about the stars and sky:

do not ask for answers from the trees and ferns
but instead try to be them,
to learn their ways

do not judge them for their slow growth.

Their growth is steady
and they know how to forgive
which is a magical quality all its own,

remember they are patient like no other.

We should be as the forest
blessed and growing
and constant.

Our power lies in each new moment,
time will not disappoint us.

Collect the light,
gather it into the bowl of your bones
keep it safe until you are at the ocean
and then spread open your hips
and birth it out again

watch bits of light
drift into the sky
and out again
undulating with the waves.

Ebb & Flow

I want to learn the language of the bees,

to create something from the cosmos
from the light we have swallowed
which is resting on our tongues.

Susan Sweetland Garay

Poverty Bend Road

The curve of the road is like
the curve of a body,
each are equally
dangerous.

I do not drive slowly.

Our world contains so many worlds
so many sizes and shapes and pieces to put together,
each combination creating something completely new.

As I move I understand that I have never been
more aware of my body, of how I feel
in it and who I am in it,
how it makes me what I am

it is so lovely and so capable
even in its imperfection.

We are not separate -
our connection is complete,
for the good and bad
and the salty
and sweet,

for those times I want to cry but can't
for those whose bodies betrayed them
for how we can bathe one another in love
and intention and healing and light

and maybe things will turn out
the way we thought they would
and maybe they will turn out so much better,

Ebb & Flow

maybe someone will still leave
and someone will still lie
and things will break and crack and decay

but from that detritus will rise something else

and we will love each other for as long as humanly possible
and the earth will love us long after that.

Muted

I watch winter's first snow
come down in giant flakes
out a second story window.

I savor it,
feel the magic of it.

The silence of the snow makes dreams feel possible.
The thick white blanket
feels like a gift,

I try to hold on to the
small strings connecting us

the roots
and fantasies
and lies
that do not change the truth.

Our roots are entwined
with misunderstandings
and muted messages
hidden amidst so many
possible meanings.

But we do not have to
take on the enormity of it all
today.

Instead, maybe take just one step closer,

that one small bit of ground
covered in moss and clover
with only a few small people in it
can be your world for a while.

Choose a piece to hold in your hand,
roll it over
grow accustomed to the
weight of it.

Take it apart
piece by piece

and see if perhaps there are
a few bits worth saving.

Rib Cage

You are protectors,
but protection is an illusion,
so where does that
leave us?

You look like a cage
but your bars
act instead as cracks
so we can live in both
shadow and light.

They give us
a place to hide

but keep the light close
so we don't have to travel far
when we begin to crave her again.

You provide a home
for the heart,

putting into words
what comes up from the belly
looking for a way out.

Learning to Sing

Lately when it's
near dark and
the coyotes come,
I have heard
the babies learning
from their mothers
how to sing.

Each off note creates
a different kind of song,
beautiful and rare
and promising.

Like the act of planting
flowers in a place that isn't
yours, where you may
never return to.

On the mornings
after these nights,
I wake wanting to
lay my cheek down
directly on the earth
and listen to what she
tells me.

Layers

We fight on a Saturday afternoon
and I feel the weekend is ruined,

but our baby plays happily
and I still smile at her brightly,
with all my might,
and I hope she can't tell
how deeply I don't feel it.

She looks to me,
as I am her gauge of
the state of things

and I won't let her down.

After the argument is over and I am alone
I think about what he told me, wondering if he is right.

We all have layers to peel away
and I suppose I still have many
of my own to get through.

Death in the Country

Out here
in this country life
we are surrounded by death.

But it is not as sad
as you would think.

It is small
and natural
and common.

On good days
it is not cruel

but not every day
is a good day.

Sometimes it brings tears
and seems horribly
unfair.

But I think it is
a good place
to learn
of it.

Where it is
usual
and small
and often feels
more forgivable.

Susan Sweetland Garay

Bones on the Brain

The whole house was sleeping
and I was sleepy too
but on that day sleep
felt like a waste of
precious time

so instead I sat on the floor
glassy eyed,
sketching skulls.

We cut through bones
yesterday evening
in the dark.

Now I have bones on the brain.

I think both
of their strength
and fragility

remembering how easily
my own have broken.

The other day a woman showed me how the
inside of a human skull has a pattern
on it that looks just like a leaf
pressed into silver.

In the crisp air and quiet of an
empty room in the early morning
it seems quite natural,
that each should be
inside the other.

Optimists Underneath

Someone tells me
that nothing is broken,

but we are all broken,
cracked, bruised and bloody –
but I see the beauty in it.
In our strength

that we keep going
day after day
after month and year.

We are all optimists underneath,

and anyway maybe our job in this
is not to try to stop the suffering
but instead to turn our focus
from ourselves,

so do not worry too much
over your broken heart

the cracks are what keep it open.
Try not to forget the beauty of the world
or of your particular life,

try to let the pain
keep you soft
and your eyes open,

let the cracks be windows
to bring in new air.

Cooking Dinner Together
in the Late Summer or Early Fall

Together we move the kitchen table outside
and walk back in with garden spoils,
zucchini and potatoes, destined
for our yellow enamel pot
already simmering on the stove.

As he cuts the peppers
he saves the seeds for next year.

He swirls the contents of the pot,
examines,
smells
and sets it back down to simmer.

We must test what we
will feed to those we love.

Susan Sweetland Garay

Unmade

Inside the sacred no is a much bigger yes

that contains discernment and digestion and
listening to your body's wisdom.

I am made of water,
as are you,
so it makes sense
for us to return
to it

so I walk outside
into the rain.

I watch my daughter play and am unmade by her,

her determination
and ability to stretch.
The clarity with which she knows what she wants
and then her ability to commit to it fully.

She does not question.

Motherhood is a kind of map making,
and for me nothing ever came all at once.

It is more gradual
a process or a
coming into knowledge

like a frightened animal
slowly creeping out
of the shadow and
into the sunlight.

Leap Day

She notices the moon
and points it out to us
asking with an open cupped hand
for us to bring it down
and hand it to her.

To her it is a reasonable request
but she does not seem overly disappointed
when we shake our heads no.

I speak to God often

and sometimes
he speaks back.

He almost always
waves hello when
the wind rustles
the leaves
on the large tree
by the driveway
and the sound is
so lovely
and noticeable
that even
my 1 ½ year old
stops her splashing
in the mud puddle
and turns to listen.

Sometimes I do what I do
(walk in the woods or write a poem)
because it's the only way
I know how to pray.

Small Corner

I sense the weirdness of time passing

and see how small
my place in the world is.
But this does not make me
feel unimportant.

I am vital to my small corner.

It could not be what it is
without me.

And that corner is plenty.

We would all like
things to be simple
but that is not really
what happens here.

I arrive home to a cool house
amidst the early summer heat,
a happy husband
marinating the chicken,
cats purring in their sleep,
a daughter playing in the grass
and bright flowers in bloom
in the front yard.

Who says this isn't magic.

I Dreamt That I Died

I dreamt last night that I died
(oh horror of horrors!)
and when I did I realized
that there is not enough evidence
in this world of how much I love you,

so let this be that evidence –

that I love you thoroughly and madly,
like the moon loves the stars
and the sky loves the birds,
like the bees love the flowers
that they spend their lives
in search of,

like the ocean loves the
sand below and the sun above,
you are both, in front of and behind me.
Above and below.

All things are here through you
and will be here because of you.
I would have little reason
to be here without you.

I love you so that no time can pass
with me existing in it
when you do not exist in me.

Susan Sweetland Garay

The First Time We Hear the Coyotes After a Long Winter

I leave the window open,
no matter how cold,
so we can hear them
as she falls asleep,
high pitched and sweet.

Later as the rest of the house sleeps
I think about each choice I have made,
what I did and what else I could have done.

Maybe if I had made another choice
things would be better, perfect even.

Or maybe we would still be here in this,
or some very similar, uncomfortable place.

So I try to listen to a friend who tells me,
you are one hell of a mother,

and this time I am glad
to be alone and awake at this hour.

I have missed this song.

Ritual

On some nights she sleeps besides me
so that I can comfort her, but
when I wake in the night
she is what
brings me back

she is how I know the difference
between what is a dream
and what is real.

Just allow the transformation
I tell myself

but there are still questions.

There will always
be questions
so when I say I know,

perhaps what I mean to say is,
my body knows.

My body, which is actually all bodies,
all space, and trees and dirt and ferns
and waves crashing.
All life.

My body whose pieces have been
around much longer than I have,
she is wiser than I am.

But happily
I get to benefit
from her wisdom if
I can learn to listen to
what she tells me.

Walks

Bless the moon in her
consistency
and cycles
and the insanity that she
brings to us all.

I wonder sometimes
why I want so badly
for there
to be a plan.
A right answer
amidst all the options.

Most choices are so much
less significant then we make them.

But I suppose I prefer to worry.

The other day I got in the car
and drove almost a full hour to
photograph something which
has been photographed at least
a million times before.

I suppose I believe
we each have a unique eye
and I wanted to know what mine would see.

I do not go on my walks
alone anymore.
Not ever.

It is always us,
exploring together.
Learning to notice.

Susan Sweetland Garay

I think how she will grow
up noticing and
watching me
notice.

Our education is two fold
as both are teacher and taught.

Some days
I'm sure
I am invisible.

But not today.

Susan Sweetland Garay

The Way

Maybe the way
is to be like both
water and fire

to flow
to never attempt
to move in a straight line
to patiently make my way through walls and rocks
slowly, over thousands of years

and then
to sometimes decide
to burn it all down.

Waning

Susan Sweetland Garay

Lantern Light

It's been getting dark,
so dark,
these days
and the cold is coming
and the sun is so hard to find.
Time feels short and particularly precious

and at times it feels easier
to hide
or pretend.

But motherhood makes pretending harder
and the desire to fight stronger

so we set down the confusion,
the tangle of emotion
we can't fully view
or understand.

We offer up what we have.

We help
and show our children
what comes from helping.

We are in a place that feels strange
and unfinished -
because truthfully
every place is strange and unfinished.

There is no changing some things.

Ebb & Flow

So we carry on.
We mother.
We create.
We plan.
We keep the world moving
with paying bills and making meals
and cleaning up all manner of messes.

We move as if one hand
was tied behind our backs.

We wait for rain,
for puddles to form,
wait for dark
and then for the magic of the moonrise.

We are such moody creatures.

Inverted

The journey we thought
would take hours
took days,

but if this inverted story arc
brought us anything, it was
a day of successful execution.

We all live in a burning building so
you can't scare me by holding up a match,

in fact give me the matches,
let us women burn it down.

The time for prayers
and patience is over.

Remove your hand from my mouth
and you will see the fire I can breathe.

Do not talk to me about patience,
do not dare tell me to wait
just a little while longer.

I have waited enough.

The universe is vast
and generous
and good

but people may not be.

We will not limit ourselves -
there will be enough for all of us.

Ebb & Flow

We will make each movement
under a strawberry moon
and watch as we
change the
world.

Susan Sweetland Garay

Orange Peels

A wise woman tells me,
make space, new ideas will come

and so I try to identify
what I no longer need.

When the world is burning,
not somewhere else but here,

and collectively we know that it will be a while
before this dark is over,

still, it is only a small shattering
and maybe the specific path does not matter

maybe orange peels in a pile in the sink
don't have to mean anything

and maybe when it feels like we are
living in a circular world

with no doors
or answers,

when there is so much fire
everywhere

inside
and out

when forward motion
feels better -

Ebb & Flow

we keep moving
as if action is the only language that matters,

maybe the hardest part
is always allowing things to die.

Needles

The slow death of winter
comes

and though I try to remain distant
I cannot help but hope,

so I lean in with a hard yes
working diligently at what I can control
and releasing what I can't.

And when the only answer
is *I just don't know,*
try to realize that
this is only our beginning.

Speak it out loud,
and then
go outside
to play in the snow.

Maybe that is the first step,
to let out a wild and authentic laugh
as I sled down the long hill of our snow
covered backyard as the moon rises.

And maybe clarity in something easy
will help bring the rest of the world into alignment,
back into the light.

Maybe we will reject these rules
and decide to make new ones,

maybe we throw away those old maps
realizing finally that we can make our own.

Messages to Myself

For weeks
I have been living
inside a large ball of grief

where pleasure and pain
and sleep and dreams
seem to mix together
and it's difficult to
tell top from bottom,

and its many sources
turn into one unintelligible beast.

I have no words for it
only a big dark hole in my insides
full of dread and anger
and hopeless sadness
and so much fear

and I want someone to tell me:
Yes. I hear you. You are not wrong.
One day it will get better,
you will not always have this hole.
One day it will fill with something
so much better.

So I tell myself.

Just wait.
Slow down.
Hold still.
Let arms wrap around you.
Let voices reach you.

Susan Sweetland Garay

Be still,
and see if it feels
any different when
you are quiet

if you can see another side
or hear a bird calling
bringing you to
another possible
path.

There are so many possibilities
dear one, so many ways
you cannot yet see.

Maybe take a walk,
breath the clean air,
speak to the trees,
the ancient ones
with so much wisdom,
speak to them and then be still
and see if they speak back.

Just try
even if it feels useless.

And when you don't know
who you can trust and you doubt
your own insides
trust the trees
and the ferns
and the mushrooms
and all those ancient growing things
that belong to the earth.

She is our mother
and she will not
steer you wrong.

A Night in Harvest

Husband and daughter sleep in the bedroom quietly
a fan blows in the other room.
It is full dark out and
the windows
are open.

I can hear the strong breeze in the leaves
that are just starting to turn.

I think sometimes that I would feel
whatever I feel
good or bad

regardless of whatever life event or circumstance
I am blaming my mood on.

I swallow disappointment
and irritation
often.

Let it go, I tell myself.

Release it
Release it
Release it

This work is surely good
for the soul and skin.

The moon was up and full this morning as I drove to work,

some truths are only found in darkness
in the cleanliness of dirt and ground and natural things
breaking down.

Susan Sweetland Garay

Hold space for detritus
and decomposition,

that is how the transformation happens

and that,
is the magic.

Icicle Creek

On a perfectly magical day at the river
your father and I were talking,
so content to be where we were,
and in our happiness didn't see you
take two steps forward on slippery rocks

and when I looked down you were
completely submerged in the clear cold water,
eyes open, mouth open, looking interested
but not at all afraid.

I scooped you out of the water
and held your wet body to mine,
wiped water from your eyes and
waited for the wail to come.

But you only smiled at me
put your head on my shoulder
and held on to my
wet red hair.

Cyclical

Lately I have found a new respect
and love for this land
in which I live.

The other night we ate an entire meal
supplied by our backyard.
I love this place I tell him.
You got that right sweets, he tells me.

In my parents backyard I find a plant,
nearly, but not yet dead, growing
out of an old cinder block
in the shade and wet
under ferns and fir trees.

Since no dirt can be found
it is sprouting roots wildly into the air
perhaps with an outlandish hope
that they will encounter earth
or some nourishing surface to grow into.

Looking out my office window
to the vines and sun
I think

how odd the connection
that can sprout out of death.

It's cyclical she tells me,
and I say
You got that right sister.

The Wet Green Forest

I am from the wet green forest,
where leaves decompose
under our feet
and moss drips
from the trees.

Where ferns grow
from the cracks
in cement walls
and it seems that
nature always wins.

In this place we
release what is
dark and thick
and smells like life

to prepare the ground around us,
so it is full of richness
from the selves that
we let fall away.

Then in the fall time
when the harvest comes
and the air turns cool,
we reap.

We dig
and eat
and dry
and enjoy
and try to make
it last for as long as possible.

Susan Sweetland Garay

We bring the colors
of the outside in.

We peel and plan
and watch the rain that
hasn't stopped falling for days.

Water makes a million tiny rivers
unconcerned about what
they may wash away.

The land is powerless
against it.

Her power
is found in
her softness,
her flexibility,
her knowing that

we are not
the center
of anything.

Distraction

On a particularly rough day,
I sit on the living room floor
with my daughter

each of us taking turns
playing and crying and
holding the other.

So we decide to
get out of the house,
though the day is dark
and grey and
full of rain.

I know right away it was the right choice.

The feel of the air
through the open car window
is enough to make us both forget
what we were crying about.

Susan Sweetland Garay

A Fast Burn or a Slow Unfolding

I open my eyes to a sunburst ceiling
and wonder if it will be a fast burn
or a slow unfolding.

A sneaker wave
that attacks when you
are not careful

catching you
unaware
and relaxed,

or if it will approach
slowly, allowing our fear
to grow as we wait for its arrival.

They tell me
to be patient,
that the roots
will reveal themselves.

But I will not waste any more time.

I am sure footed as I walk away.

The Ferns

Two days ago I was so lucky
as to take a walk in the woods
at the precise moment when
every fern in the forest was unfurling.

Each step brought new wonder
and I could hardly bring myself
to leave.

There is a mythology
rooted in this land,

not just in the minds
of those who live here

but in the land itself.

It grows stronger with
each new growing thing

and I feel privileged to witness it.

I look at our lawn and
secretly I love the weeds
even as they have taken
over our yard and almost
outnumber the blades of grass -

I love them.

Susan Sweetland Garay

I love the wildflowers
who do not come up in orderly beds
and have no proper place,
but simply burst forth
and blossom wherever
they like.

I fight against the
extension of my world,
preferring it small and green
and with very little asphalt.

There will be time to push tomorrow,
but for tonight, I will just
ask for mercy from the
earth and sky

and remember the ferns.

Chapel

These days my chapel
on Sunday is a dark wood,
damp and growing,

or the ocean in constant motion
with its familiar sound
calming all who
come near it.

God's creations
not man's
are where
we worship.

Susan Sweetland Garay

Eclipse Season

Eclipse season comes
and everything in the world
conspires to remind me
to surrender.

To soften
into the path
that was chosen for me.

When I was young
I went to Sunday school
every Sunday
and they gave us
answer after answer
to all sorts of very hard questions.

Now on Sunday mornings
we make pancakes together
and go out into the green or blue
of the world

and when my daughter asks
me difficult questions
I tell her the truth,

that I don't know the answer for sure
but that maybe I have a belief
or a hope, that maybe the
important part is
exploring deeper into
the questions and
into ourselves.

Dreaming of the Dead and Not Yet Born

I am a gatherer of bones
who finds stories and
then tries to remember them.

I have some of yours
kept close

and now you're gone from this world
and you were gone
for me
long before that -
but I cannot remember why.

Sometimes it feels
like floating
or flying
or falling

but sometimes power comes
from giving in
or leaving behind.

Now I am afraid
but my fear and the
ever present eventual goodbye
make the creating feel more vital

and so on a day when the
anger is all
encompassing

I imagine you both nearby
walking barefoot over rocks
and dipping toes
into cold water

Susan Sweetland Garay

listening and
waiting
patiently
for your turn.

And when I think I am alone
driving through the dark,
that I am the only one,

I remember that we are never the only ones,

and when it is time to step away
I turn my back quickly
and even that
small movement
begins to bring relief.

Underwater Life

We began
by dancing with
our eyes closed

and it
became much
easier after that.

In the bath her
hair swirls around
her angelic face.
She is still and serene
for longer than I expect.

Her face begins to
curve into a smile,
eyes still closed,
hair still a swirl
of seaweed or
underwater life
around her.

Susan Sweetland Garay

Sun Break

Today it rained for
7 hours straight I think
and then abruptly cleared
to a lovely blue sky and
magical quality of light
that you can never
quite capture in
a picture.

So the two of us
hurriedly threw on
our jackets and ran out
the door so as not to
miss our chance.

West

An odd old man in Idaho
gave me a painting once
which I loved
and carried with me
through many states
for many years
until I left it
on the wall
of my very small home
as I packed my life
into a medium sized car
to travel West,

where people have always gone
when they want to begin again.

I spend my moments attempting to
teach others to see me
and trying like hell to let them
be who they really are.

Let us not be vague,
a foggy tree line partly hidden,
a line dotted and unsure.

Just put the brush to the paper
and see what appears.

I spy a lady bug on some tall grass
and carefully pick her up and place her in my hand
I admire her as she crawls over fingers and palm,

then it's time for her to fly away
but her first attempt fails
with sticky wings that don't spread
as they should.
She is grounded
again and
again,

till her fourth attempt
when her execution is flawless.

Blank Pages

Snow covers this place
like an answer to a question
I didn't know I'd been asking.

It washes away more
than the rain can.
Leaving only
blank pages
waiting to have
their story rewritten.

I once stole two rocks from
the Zen rock garden in my
therapist's office because I
thought carrying them with me
might bring clarity or strength -

perhaps they helped,
perhaps not.

My stubbornness takes many
who used to know me by surprise,
but there is no shame in fragility and I
won't be taken over by
illusions now.

Words are powerful.

I say it out loud
as I sit down and
begin writing.

Susan Sweetland Garay

Breakfast

We sit together eating eggs
with messy hair and sleepy eyes.

She watches with her new eyes
and tastes her food happily.

I think to myself that this,
right here, is reason
enough.

Listening

I watch two electric blue dragonflies
frolic near a bush full of magenta berries
next to where I sit on the damp grass.
One stops for a while
and before he leaves
I study the patterns in his
iridescent wings.

Don't run from distraction he tells me,
embrace the surprising unknowns.
Play.

For me
it comes in bits and pieces
and requires a lot of rearranging.

I walk outside to ask
the land what she would like to tell me,
what I need to know,
on a misty morning when water
seems to float in the air

and as I walk my eye immediately goes to
a gloriously enormous slug in shades
of ochre and grey with a
mountain range
of ridges on
his back.

He travels slowly
but his movement is steady
and I have no doubt that he will get where
he is going.

Susan Sweetland Garay

The sun is warm on my back.
I hear bees buzzing nearby and

I don't know if the land is listening
but I say thank you just in case.

Tracks

Yesterday on our walk
I took a photograph of
tire tracks left in the mud.
They were not extraordinary
and I wondered why I stopped,
what pulled me there.

I am not
particularly
extraordinary
I think to myself
looking at my
messy desk and
empty coffee cup

but I still like
when someone
stops to notice
me.

4th of July

Darkness is coming
so we gather wood
on the beach to
build our fire.

The flames are lovely and
though we are not alone here,
we might as well be.

The darkness protects us.

We light leftover fireworks
one by one throwing them
towards the water
in the dark
watching as they spin
and burn out.

Then our ordinary show
becomes remarkable
when a wave coming closer
with the incoming tide
takes one, still lit, and
carries it toward the sea.

It is still spinning as it floats away.

Ebb & Flow

The Next Phase

I sit back and watch as the unreal becomes real,
horrors become usual,
and outrage begins to fade.

Responsibility is not a negative,
a dirty word
to be avoided.

I am both here and not here.

Grief makes it more real
and less,
I don't know
what comes next.

The moon was full last night
as we stepped out into the cold

this will be our last
time seeing the moon
over this particular field and hills.

I mourn it
but I am ready
to move to the
next phase.

Reuse could be the battle cry
for this generation
and the next

I am confident
that overall we are
getting smarter,

Susan Sweetland Garay

we must be
I tell myself
as I watch two boys
at preschool chase each other
around with plastic saws.
The teacher calls after them,
"it's not a weapon,
it's for building things."

They continue on in their game.

Reason Enough

We found deer bones once
in the grove of trees behind ours house
that had already been cleaned by the coyotes,

two rabbits as well and
a small graveyard of mice
and other rodents
left by the cats.

Nature is odd in its
giving
and taking

so when you are losing faith do not forget
that good for the sake of good
is reason enough,

and know
that even this grief
will bring
creation
of something.

All Directions

I am out of balance
my roar and my whisper -
both feel neglected and so
come forward yelling whenever
they see the opportunity.

We are always both alive and dead,
here and far away.

I want to walk on my toes
to bend
and stretch
in all directions.

I need lightness
and open roads

and on the days when
there are no maps
we go the way
that feels
like the way
we should go.

The way of our bones
and belly's
that feels like
blueberries on a
summer day,
right and delicious.

Comfort

We wonder what can comfort us now
and so she tells us where to begin:

Be comforted by your creations
by the dirty process
of putting pieces together
of arranging
and cleaning
and throwing away
and starting again.

Be comforted by the earth
and her chaos and creation
and death and life
and being held by her.

Be comforted by yourself,
reminded of your strength
and of where you've been,
who you have become.

Be comforted by the letting go
the knowing that you were
right to bury it in the earth
by knowing that you
can trust in your choice
of what to destroy.

Wind Storm

The wind raged outside
when we woke up
this morning

but it did not
feel angry,

perhaps instead
she was showing us
her power

through her lament
for the broken ground around us
and all of our children who did not go to sleep safe and warm.

The wind blows hard
and I watch the petals fall
from our magnificent magnolia

and I feel somehow cleaner
than I did before.

Sunrise

Awake as the sun rises
I step out onto the porch
searching for cool air.

The color red bursts through
my closed eyes.

Soon full daylight will come
proclaiming against
the dark

but for now I enjoy
the cool and darkness.

The sunrise is the color of berries,
and like blood it greedily spreads
not wanting to leave anything
unstained.

Ask

That first day it was a comfort
having you with me,
with us,
for a little while longer.

But it changed after that.

I ask how to heal
and am told to find joy,
make joy,
radiate it.
Don't doubt its power.

While still in it
I try to make a plan
to force a path to open up
before me

I know it won't work,
they warn me it won't work,
that it is too soon,
but still I try.

Each time I am finally
beautifully
alone
I immediately
drop the performance
and am overcome.

Ebb & Flow

I think of you
who belongs with us
who is a part of us already
who should be here
who we longed for
and worked for
and waited for,
how can you not be here?

As I am momentarily thinking about something else
another wave washes over me
the air leaves my lungs
while my mind fills

and when I can breathe again
the release of tears
feels almost pleasurable.

It would have been so easy
to fall into a deep dark hole.

I ask
what do I do now?

And I am answered
you fly,
you rise,
you become stronger.
You do all things that you have awlays done
better then you have ever
done them before.

Susan Sweetland Garay

The Necessity of Rage

I am tired of building walls
to protect my tender heart.

Instead
I want to get angry.

To allow my fury for all
that is wrong with this world.

They tell me
to calm down

but I know
how to tell
the truth from a lie,
and I will not be calm.

I will not be nice.

I will be as loud as I like
for as long as I like.

I am the difficult woman.

Our children will inherit this world
and so we go to work to make it worth giving.

I will not apologize for strength
or truth telling.

Ebb & Flow

We each feel a full rainbow of emotion
forgetting in the moment that they are each a gift.
Forgetting the feeling of going years without
the release of a good solid cry,
without so many portions of a truthful life,

and truthfully we cannot be powerfully anything
without being truthful.

Something angry is
trying to crawl out through my mouth,
livid at having to escape instead of being set free.

The wind is getting colder
but we are not afraid of a bit of blood,
and so we will all be back tomorrow.

Susan Sweetland Garay

Speak up

This is the thing I want to say:

when I was young
I never knew that there was
more than one path open to us,
that we could make the difficult choice

but I want you
to know it.

Sometimes I don't know how to do
the thing that I have to do,
the thing that I have chosen.

Sometimes my
skin feels inside out
and my body like it is in 12
places at once.

Sometimes I try to tell someone
something, anything,
but I am behind glass.

No one can hear me.
No one can see my face
without a blur hiding its detail.

Lately I am a calm sea
quiet, with slow, constant motion,
but no release.

Ebb & Flow

The small waves
are lulling me into a trance
that will take me through
the long days of darkness
and winter and waiting

but this false calm
cannot last.

I am ready now
to show my
true face.

I am made of fire and earth
and they do not hide.

I look around and see
so many others walking upstream

and I wonder why we keep
trying to exert ourselves
over things clearly
so much more
powerful than
we are.

Susan Sweetland Garay

Quench

The heat of summer intrudes
into everything

my anger burns hotter
and never quite quenches

no matter how many bodies of water
I find to lower myself into.

I want to
learn to be better
than I am
than I think I can be.

The world is falling apart
again

though I know really it never stopped

and tomorrow when we leave
on yet another journey
the moon is coming
with us.

In this new space
I feel cooler, with
more shades of blue
more calm
slower
and with space
to pause.

Ebb & Flow

I want cold water
cooling and quenching

so we travel
to a mighty lake
with frigid waters.
We find a place where
she shares her coolest parts,
from the deepest of her depths,
with a dry, burning world

and we peel off our layers
and step joyfully in.

Acknowledgements

A Fast Burn or a Slow Unfolding – Vox Poetica
A Night in Harvest – Analekta Anthology, 2016-2017
Ancient Corners – Tiny Poetry
Bones on the Brain – Analekta Anthology, 2016-2017
Chapel - The Art of Being Human vol 15
Comfort - Winedrunk Sidewalk: Shipwrecked in Trumpland, Women's History Month
Death in the Country - The Galway Review
Distraction – The Galway Review
Dreaming of the Dead and the Not Yet Born – Fourth & Sycamore, 2nd Publicarion; Blue Hour Anthology Volume 4
Ebb and Flow – Analekta Anthology, 2016-2017
First Birthday - Leaves of Ink
Generations – Leaves of Ink
Go Softly – Leave of Ink
Grandfather - Leaves of Ink
Icicle Creek – Pyrokinection Journal
Inverted - Kind of a Hurricane Press, Emergence Anthology (print)
Lantern Light – Vox Poetica
Layers – Hart Poetry Contest
Leap Day – Analekta Anthology, 2016-2017
Learning to Sing – Analekta Anthology Volume 2, 2014
Listening – Vox Poetica
Muted – Emerge Magazine
Needles - Fourth & Sycamore
Orange Peels – Blue Hour Anthology Volume 4
Pinpricks – Boned
Poverty Bend Road – Vox Poetrica
Putting the Baby to Sleep - Leaves of Ink
Quench - Winedrunk Sidewalk: Shipwrecked in Trumpland, Women's History Month
Reason Enough - Poetry of the Resistance

Rib Cage – Vox Poetica
Rise – Poetry of the Resistance
Skin - Zoomoozophone Review Issue 5
Small Corner - Sagittarius Anthology
Speak Up – Blue Hour Anthology Volume 4
The Continuity of Things – Tiny Poetry
The Ferns - Zoomoozophone Review
The First Time We Hear the Coyotes After a Long Winter-
    Pyrokinection Journal
The Necessity of Rage – Vox Poetica
The Next Phase - Winedrunk Sidewalk: Shipwrecked in
    Trumpland
The Way - Poetry of the Resistance
The Wet Green Forest - Leaves of Ink
Tracks – East Jasmine Review
Unearth – The Lake
Unmade - The Art of Being Human Volume15
Walks – Camel Saloon
West - Kind of a Hurricane Press, Emergence Anthology (print)
Wind Storm - Leave of Ink

Bio

Born and raised in Portland Oregon, Susan Sweetland Garay received a Bachelor's degree in English Literature from Brigham Young University, spent some years in the Ohio Appalachians and currently lives in the Willamette Valley with her husband and daughter where she works in the vineyard industry and enjoys small town living.

She enjoys finding beauty and meaning in the everyday. She has had poetry and photography published in a variety of journals, online and in print. Her first full length poetry collection, *Approximate Tuesday*, was published in 2013 and she was nominated for a Pushcart Prize in 2014. Her second book, *Strange Beauty,* was published by Aldrich Press in 2015.

She is a founding editor of The Blue Hour Press. More of her work can be found at studiorainwater.org.

www.ingramcontent.com/pod-product-compliance
Lightning Source LLC
Chambersburg PA
CBHW020428010526
44118CB00010B/478